the natives guide working in ski resorts

Edited by

Iain Martin
Vicky Brown

First published 2003

Edited by Iain Martin & Vicky Brown
Design by Obok (obokdesign@aol.com)
Reprographics by Skonto, Krakow, Poland
Printing by Drukarnia Skleniarz, Krakow, Poland

Published by Natives.co.uk Ltd
39-43 Putney High St
London SW15 1SP
Tel – 08700 463377

ISBN 0-9545625-0-X

Thanks to Duncan, Neil, Leslie, Rich and Jan for your support and encouragement

contents

photo credits

Front/Back Cover:
© Red Bull Snowthrill of Alaska,
Photographer: Dan Ferrer, Rider: Guerlain Chicherit

p5 © Salomon Sports, Rider: Jim Adlington
p6 © Henry Meredith, Rider: Mark Harris
p8 Photographer: Gail Cargill (top right)
p9 © Inghams Travel (bottom left)
p10 © Inghams Travel
p12 Photographer: Tom Greenall (bottom right)
Rider: Ian Hopper (top right)
p13 © Inghams Travel
p15 © Inghams Travel (centre)
© Salomon Sports, Rider: Jim Adlington
p19 © Salomon Sports, Rider: Jim Adlington
p20 Rider: Dan Botham
p21 Rider: Dan Botham
p22 © Photographer: Henry Meredith, Rider: Mark Harris
p24 © Red Bull Snowthrill of Alaska,
Photographer: Jean-Marc Farve, Rider: Jamie Burge
p26 Photographer: Gail Cargill
p27 Rider: Robert Muir
p28 © Inghams Travel
p30 Photographer: Marie-France Goddard
p31 Photographer: Marie-France Goddard (top right)
p32 Boarders: Tim Chamberlain/Ian West, Skier: Euan Cormack
p33 © Red Bull Snowthrill of Alaska,
Photographer: Christian Pondella, Rider: Chris Davenport
Photographer: Gail Cargill (top right)
p34 © Red Bull Snowthrill of Alaska,
Photographer: Christian Pondella, Rider: Sverre Liliequist
p37 © Salomon Sports, Rider: Jim Adlington
p38 © Henry Meredith, Rider: Mark Harris
p41 © PGL Travel
p44 © Red Bull Snowthrill of Alaska,
Photographer: Dan Ferrer, Rider: Sverre Liliequist
p46 Skier: Iain Martin
p47 Photographer: Robert Muir, Parapenter: Susie Burt
p48 Photographer: Gail Cargill

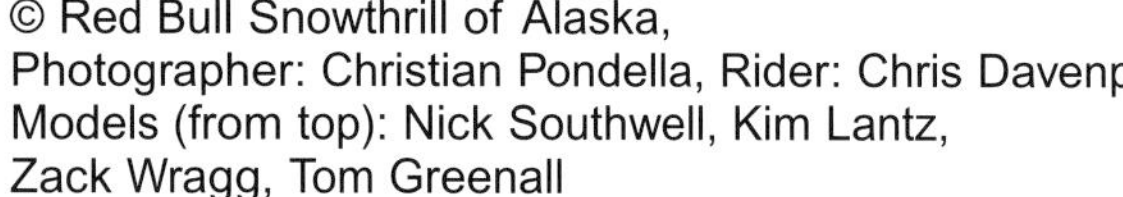

p49 © Kevin Turner (top right)
Photographer: Gail Cargill (centre)
p50 © Red Bull Snowthrill of Alaska,
Photographer: Christian Pondella, Rider: Chris Davenport
p60 Models (from top): Nick Southwell, Kim Lantz,
Zack Wragg, Tom Greenall

Natives would like to thank Cordula at Red Bull Photofiles for all her help in providing their great shots.

natives.co.uk
knowledge is powder

the natives guide to working in ski resorts

Why do a season?

Every winter thousands of young Brits head off to the snow to spend their winter in ski resorts.

The fact that you are even reading this now means that you have something in common with all those saisonniers who have passed on or given up 'real jobs' to choose life.

Doing a ski season is life affirming. It can't be valued in monetary terms. How do you place a value on experiences you'll never forget and friends you'll keep for the rest of your life?

Since Natives first launched four years ago, we've been able to help thousands of people fulfill their dream of working in a ski resort.

As the industry specialists, we have published the Natives Guide to Working in Ski Resorts so you can find out more about how to enjoy a season yourself and how to get the most out of it.

We will guide you through what the season is all about, from the jobs available, how to get them, what to do if you don't want to work, and how to survive before, during and after the season.

And what is a season like? Only natives of the mountains really know, but over the next sixty pages we'll use our insider knowledge to reveal all...

A brief history of Natives:

Natives.co.uk started as a project by founder Iain Martin, who was fed up with season workers being misrepresented in so-called 'documentaries' on TV. The website launched in the heat of the dot.com boom in April 1999. Traffic soon grew and has continued to grow as season workers, job seekers and informed riders alike have come to the site.

Now Natives serves over 400,000 page impressions a month to more than 50,000 unique users, making it the UK's leading snowsports lifestyle website. More season workers get their jobs through Natives than any other source.
Our new site - ResortJobs.co.uk – is now beginning to take on the same role for summer work.

which job?

So you've taken the first step, and decided that you'd like to work in a ski resort - now all you have to decide is which position to go for....

There are a number of different jobs available, ranging from traditional positions such as Chalet Host and Resort Rep, to specialist positions such as Ski/Snowboard Instructor, Massage Therapist, and Accountant.

The following chapter is a user-friendly guide to what's available, featuring job descriptions, package details, and pros and cons for each position from an insider's point of view.

But before you read on, have a think about what you want to gain from the season - are you looking for the position which, for example;

- offers maximum time on the slopes?
- allows for the best social life?
- offers career progression?
- improves language skills?

You should also take a realistic look at your skills and experience, in relation to those required for each position, and decide which job suits you best.

Don't forget that it may be possible to add to your skills by taking a specialised course, for example a cookery, ski technician or instructor course, or by attending one of our Job Workshops.

Most importantly, don't despair! Regardless of your priorities, skills, or experience, as long as you are willing, able, and enthusiastic, there will be something to suit you!

Chalet Host

When the concept of the 'chalet holiday' was first introduced, this position was fondly known as 'chalet girl', and was generally filled by young females who were able to perform minor miracles in tiny kitchens, and who were notorious for working hard and playing hard!

Times have moved on, however, and as a result of the ever-expanding chalet market, the chalet host/rep/cook/boy/girl (job titles differ across companies) position now offers the highest number of vacancies, and is filled by males, females, and couples, from the age of 18 right up to 50's, all with varied experience and background.

Duties

The role typically involves the provision of breakfast, afternoon tea, and a three-course dinner with wine for groups of up to twelve guests. In addition, responsibilities will include keeping the chalet clean, general guest welfare, and budgeting/shopping/food orders.

Chalets range in size from 6 to 40-bed properties, and many companies also run larger 'Club Hotels'. Generally, chalet hosts work alone, although for larger chalets, assistants are employed, giving the host more responsibility.

Skills Required

Most companies do not require formal qualifications, although previous catering experience is preferred. Many cookery schools now offer courses specific to running a chalet – if you have no catering experience, this is a great way to develop your skills and will significantly increase your chances of securing a position. Take a look in 'Getting the Job' for more info on cookery courses.

When applying, you will usually be required to submit a menu plan (see 'Menu Planning' p.29). Many companies will also test your cooking abilities at interview stage.

Working Hours

This particular position is hard work, with lots of early starts (0700/0730, 6 days per week), often demanding guests, and many hours during the season with toilet brush in hand, cleaning loos – it is by no means glamorous!

However, once a routine is established, it does offer lots of time on the slopes (from 1100 to 1600 is quite achievable) and one day off per week in which to recover/ski/board!

Package

Wages range from £50 per week to £130 per week, depending on the company, and levels of catering and service required. The package always includes food (your own cooking!), accommodation (can be in chalet or in separate shared apartment), lift pass, equipment hire, and return travel to resort from the UK.

If you do a good job guests will generally tip well. There are other ways of supplementing your income, such as a chalet 'bar' (offering bottled beers, soft drinks, and chocolate bars to guests, run on an honesty basis) and packed lunches, but these depend on local laws and your employer's policy.

Pros & Cons

- ✔ Guests buying you drinks / offering jobs
- ✔ Marriage proposals
- ✔ Good tips
- ✔ Lots of time on the mountain
- ✔ Ways to make extra cash

- ✘ Dish-pan hands
- ✘ Cleaning toilets
- ✘ Early alarm calls
- ✘ Open-plan kitchens with nowhere to hide!

CHEF

It is much easier for anyone with professional chef qualifications to find work in a ski resort, with positions available in chalets and Club Hotels as well as in bars/restaurants.

Many of the luxury chalet operators will only employ fully qualified chefs, due to the standard of catering required.

In Club Hotels, the larger numbers catered for (up to 200 guests) mean a demand for experienced Head Chefs, with Assistant and Sous Chef positions available for more recently qualified applicants.

Duties

As Chalet Chef, duties are largely the same as those of a chalet host, with more emphasis on menu planning, stock control and budgeting. A very high standard of catering is required.

Usually a chalet host/assistant(s) will be employed to work alongside you, and will carry out the other chalet duties, such as serving meals, cleaning and general guest welfare.

In larger chalets and Club Hotels, additional duties may include:

- Planning and costing of weekly menus
- Stock-control
- Control of food budgets, in conjunction with the Hotel or Chalet Manager
- Management of a team of kitchen staff
- Ensuring health & hygiene standards met
- Creation and design of special menus based on theme or regional influence

Skills Required

There are positions available for all grades of chef, with relevant qualifications including City and Guilds 706/1 and 706/2, NVQ Levels 2/3 Catering, and equivalent.

Working Hours

In a chalet or Club Hotel, your working hours will be similar to those of a chalet host, as lunch is not served to guests. So once routines are established, there will be lots of time to spend on the slopes during the day, with one full day off per week.

Bear in mind though that some Club Hotels in good locations open up their terrace for lunchtime business. Working in one of these locations, or in a locally owned bar/restaurant, will usually mean a shift system, with a mixture of day and evening shifts in any single week, with one full day off.

Package

Wages range from £90 - £200 per week, depending on the company and the responsibilities held. Packages usually include food, accommodation (can be in chalet or in separate shared apartment), lift pass, equipment hire, insurance and return travel to resort from the UK.

Good chefs working in chalets can expect to be tipped well by the guests. Tips in Club Hotels tend to get shared around all the staff. As with chalet hosts, there may be acceptable ways of supplementing your income, depending on local laws and the policy of your employer.

Pros & Cons

✔ Higher pay
✔ No washing up / cleaning toilets
✔ Opportunity for creativity

✘ No guest contact
✘ More responsibility
✘ Can mean lunchtime work

Resort Rep

You may have seen reps featuring on various 'fly on the wall' documentaries, and think it looks like one big party, but the reality is somewhat different. There is plenty of work involved, and the role requires endless amounts of patience and tolerance, as well as a sense of humour!

Duties

The job can vary across different companies, but the main emphasis will always be on guest care, and you will be the main point of contact for a group of guests throughout their stay.

Duties include airport transfers (generally by coach, although with smaller operators, you may actually drive the guests by minibus), organisation and purchase of lift passes, equipment hire and ski school, planning and implementation of an après-ski programme, and last but by no means least, problem solving!

Ski/board hosting/guiding – showing guests around the slopes and accompanying them for the day - can also be a large part of the rep's role. The extent of hosting required/allowed will depend on local regulations, which can change on an annual basis, and sometimes during the season itself.

Skills Required

Most positions require good conversational skills in a second European language, typically French, German or Italian. Other than that, you will need an outgoing personality, excellent communication and organisational skills, and the ability to work either alone or as part of a team.

Relevant experience in a customer service environment is also useful.

Where ski/board hosting is part of the role, you will need previous skiing/boarding experience (minimum 10 weeks) and will be competent on all levels of terrain.

Minimum age tends to be around 23.

Working Hours

This position can involve long working hours, which tend to change on a daily basis depending on what problems arise! Transfer day is typically a very long day, although this is the case for most resort staff.

Most reps will work 6 days per week, which in reality becomes seven as you often don't have an official day off, and are always at the end of a mobile phone in case of emergency (which crops up more often than you might imagine!).

Package

Wages can range from £80 - £150 week, with commission usually paid on sales of lift passes, equipment hire, ski school and après-ski. The actual pay structure varies widely from tour operator to tour operator and it can be difficult to compare, especially as some employers pay a substantial ad-hoc end of season bonus.

The package will include food (you may be required to dine with guests in chalets), accommodation (usually in separate shared apartment or your own apartment for senior roles), lift pass, equipment hire, insurance and return travel to resort from the UK.

Pros & Cons

- ✔ No toilets to scrub
- ✔ Varied hours
- ✔ Skiing or boarding can count as work

- ✘ 18-hr transfer days
- ✘ Answering same questions every week
- ✘ Being 'on call' 24/7

RESORT MANAGER

A common misconception is that resort managers ski or board all the time, while their staff slog it out down in resort, but again, the reality is somewhat different, with long hours typical of the job.

As with all management positions, this can be challenging, yet is also rewarding, with more opportunity for career enhancement.

Duties

Responsible for the smooth running of all aspects of the resort operation, you will be required to manage a team of resort staff (varying in size from 10-100), ensuring motivation of the team as well as monitoring individual performance.

Regular duties include liaison with local suppliers, completion of reports, accounts paperwork, monitoring standards, and dealing with problematic guest situations.

As with resort reps, ski hosting/guiding may be part of the role, showing guests around the ski area and accompanying them for the day, although this is less likely in a resort manager position than in a resort rep position.

Skills Required

Previous management experience is essential, as is either fluency or good conversational skills in a second European language. You will also need excellent organisational skills, and a calm, unflappable nature.

Where ski hosting is part of the role, you will need previous skiing/boarding experience (minimum 10 weeks) and will be competent on all levels of terrain.

Minimum age tends to be around 25.

Working Hours

As with resort rep, hours vary from day to day, and can be long, but on those sweet occasions when all is calm in resort you will be able to spend time on the mountain.

You will have more flexibility than other staff members as to when you work. If you spy a good powder day coming up, you may be able to do your paperwork the night before and hit the mountain for an hour in the morning.

However, don't expect to get as much time on the mountain as your staff. Senior resort managers often don't get on the slopes until after Christmas and then only once or twice a week at the most.

Generally you will have one official day off, though this is unlikely for the first month of the season, and even then, you will always be at the end of a mobile phone in case of emergency – expect the unexpected!

Package

Wages range from £100 - £250 week, depending on level of responsibility. In most cases, commission is paid on lift passes, equipment hire and ski school. Where no commission is paid, wages will be at the higher end of the scale. An end of season bonus is also often a substantial part of your remuneration.

Packages include food (you may be required to dine with guests in chalets), accommodation (usually own room or apartment), lift pass, equipment hire, insurance, and return travel to resort from the UK. It may also include a car and mobile phone for company use.

Pros & Cons

- ✔ Potential career progression
- ✔ Enhance language skills
- ✔ Higher wages

- ✘ Can end up being staff agony aunt/uncle!
- ✘ Long hours
- ✘ Being 'on call' 24/7

HOTEL MANAGER

Many of the larger ski companies operate 'Club Hotels', which range in size from 30-200 beds, and offer the informality of a chalet holiday, but in a hotel environment.

Club Hotels are usually previously French run hotels that have been taken over by a British tour operator and are fully British staffed to deal with only British guests. No local bookings will be taken.

The role of hotel manager can be challenging, but at the same time rewarding and with more career prospects than many of the other jobs.

Duties

The hotel manager is responsible for all aspects of the smooth operation of the property.

Duties include the training and management of large teams of staff, quality control, supervision of menu-planning and budgeting, liaison with local suppliers, ensuring Health and Safety regulations are adhered to, and completion of relevant paperwork and accounts.

Skills Required

Previous experience in the hotel industry is essential, as well as management experience, excellent organisational and administrative skills, and lots of enthusiasm!

Fluency in a second European language, or a good working knowledge is essential.

Minimum age tends to be around 25.

Working Hours

This is another position with varying working hours, which can potentially be very long.

It is likely that you will be on emergency call out at all times during the week, and less likely that you will have an official day off, although there will still be opportunities to spend time on the mountain.

Package

Weekly wages range from around £175 - £250, depending on level of responsibility. Typically most employers offer a performance related bonus, paid at the end of the season.

Packages include food, accommodation, lift pass, equipment hire, insurance and return travel to resort from the UK.

Pros & Cons

- ✔ Front of House guest contact
- ✔ Potential career progression
- ✔ Varied hours

- ✘ Being 'on call' 24/7
- ✘ Lots of admin and accounts
- ✘ Long hours

Chalet & Hotel Assistant/ Plongeur

In larger chalets and Club Hotels, assistants are employed to work alongside chalet hosts and chefs to perform a number of general tasks.

The position can fall under a wide range of titles, some sounding more glamorous than others, including housekeeper, host/ess ('hostie'), 'floater', MSP (Mobile Support Person) and EPH (Extra Pair of Hands)

A plongeur is the industry term for 'washer-up', also known in posh circles as a Kitchen Porter, and is simultaneously the least and most glamorous position in the Alps.

Duties

Assistant roles involve service of meals, cleaning, washing-up, assisting with food preparation, snow clearing and exterior cleaning.

You may be based in one particular chalet/club hotel or you may have a 'floating' role, where you are not assigned to a particular property, but will move around the resort as required.

Plongeurs are usually based in Club Hotels, working in a closed kitchen, with little guest contact. You may also assist with food prep, shopping, and snow clearing.

Skills Required

The good news is that you do not need lots of skills or experience for any of these roles.

Any previous hospitality experience will strengthen your application, though it is more important that you are seen to be outgoing, flexible and hard working, with bags of enthusiasm. Minimum age for all positions tends to be 18.

Working Hours

Hours are similar to those of a chalet host, with early starts (0700/0730, 6 days per week), evening work, and one full day off per week.

Although at times you may feel like a general dogsbody, these positions offer most time on the slopes, as well as the least responsibility, and you can rest easy knowing that most of your colleagues probably envy you!

Package

This is the downside – wages are roughly £40 - £60 week, plus food (usually leftovers!), accommodation (can be in chalet or in separate shared apartment), lift pass, equipment hire, insurance and return travel to resort from the UK.

Tips are generally shared among chalet and hotel staff, so you will have a little extra on top of your wages.

Pros & Cons

- ✔ Maximum time on the mountain
- ✔ Little responsibility
- ✔ Little experience required

- ✘ Low wages
- ✘ Early alarm calls
- ✘ End up doing tasks no one else wants to do

Nanny

With more and more tour operators offering crèche facilities to ensure that those with young families don't miss their annual skiing holiday, there is an ever-increasing demand for qualified nannies.

Although the position is often associated with a reputation for partying, it actually carries a lot of responsibility, and most tour operators conform to UK childcare legislation. The role is demanding but also fun, and nannies benefit from practising their chosen career in a stunning environment.

Duties

The role involves the care of children aged from 4 months up to around 5 years. This includes the planning and implementation of a stimulating activity programme, as well as ensuring a safe and hygienic nursery environment.

In addition, you are responsible for providing food and drinks throughout the day, ensuring all dietary requirements and parents' requests are adhered to.

You may be expected to carry out additional duties, for example babysitting, hosting evening meals, and assisting with airport transfers.

Skills Required

You must possess a relevant childcare qualification, either NNEB, BTEC, NVQ level 2/3 or equivalent. Some companies will also employ qualified teachers and paediatric nurses for nursery nurse positions.

There are also senior positions available, for example Head Nanny or Nursery Supervisor – for these you will need to have previous supervisory experience in the field of childcare.

Minimum age is 18 – most companies will employ newly qualified nannies.

Working Hours

Most work is during the daytime, although some companies operate shift systems to allow for the occasional morning or afternoon off. In any one week, you will have one full day off, and may work up to two evenings.

This position doesn't allow for much skiing or boarding time, although you will have the opportunity to spend lots of time outdoors, and will have just as much of a ski tan!

Package

Wages can range from £100 - £200 week. Packages include food, accommodation (can be in chalet, separate shared apartment and occasionally in the crèche itself!), lift pass, equipment hire, insurance, and return travel to resort from the UK.

It may be possible to supplement your income with private babysitting, but this will depend on local laws and your employer's policy.

Pros & Cons

- ✔ Evenings off
- ✔ Higher wages
- ✔ Building snowmen can count as work!

- ✘ Less time on the mountain
- ✘ The sound of crying babies
- ✘ Dirty nappies, sickness and other nasties!

Maintenance Staff

Reputed for never being around when needed, the 'handyman' or 'maintenance man' (or 'person' if you will) is alleged to have the easiest life of all in a ski resort.

Due to the nature of the role, however, hours can be very unpredictable, and when there are no repairs to be done, it is not unusual to be given a host of other tasks that no one else wants to do!

Duties

First and foremost, responsibilities include maintenance of all properties in either one or several resorts, including chalets and staff accommodation.

Other duties may include resort driving duties, such as luggage transfers, food and wine deliveries, and laundry distribution, as well as snow clearing and assisting in chalets on hosts' day off.

You may also be required to drive to and from the airport on transfer day.

Skills Required

Previous experience in a relevant trade such as plumbing, electrics, mechanics, or carpentry is usually required, or at the very least significant DIY and decorating experience.

A flexible nature is very important, as well as the ability to work independently, using your own initiative. A full, clean driving licence is also required.

Minimum age ranges from 21 – 24, depending on employer.

Working Hours

It is difficult to pre-determine hours for this position, although if resort driving duties are part of the role, then you will probably have a set routine, and if you cover several resorts, you may find yourself spending a lot of time driving.

Repairs are best done when there are no guests around, so it is quite normal to arrive in a chalet just after breakfast, polish off the leftovers, then set about the task in hand!

If you are up to date with tasks, then there should be plenty of time for skiing/boarding.

Transfer day is a very busy day, with repairs to be done, lightbulbs to replace, vacuum cleaners to mend (because the chalet host hasn't changed the bag all season) as well as lots of fetching and carrying, and possibly a return drive to the airport.

Package

Wages range from £60 to £100 week. Packages include food (raiding chalet fridges while doing the rounds!), accommodation (can be in chalet or separate shared apartment), lift pass, equipment hire, insurance, and return travel to resort from the UK.

Pros & Cons

- ✔ Ability to manage own time
- ✔ Lots of time on the mountain
- ✔ May be able to ski in several resorts

- ✘ Blocked toilets and other nasties
- ✘ End up doing tasks no one else wants to do
- ✘ No way of supplementing income

Bar Staff

This is probably the most desired position in any ski resort – from the outside it looks very glamorous and lots of fun. The reality is that, yes, it can be a fun position, but is also hard work, with long and tiring shifts requiring lots of energy.

As well as resort bars, there are also positions available with tour operators, in their Club Hotel bars.

Overall, there are far, far fewer positions available than the number of people looking for them, and competition is understandably high. Be prepared to apply for other jobs as well if it doesn't work out, and if you are dead-set on bar work, make sure you really sell yourself when applying!

Duties

Responsibilities include service of drinks (and sometimes food), stock control and ordering, organising après-ski events, accounting and paperwork, and maintaining cleanliness and hygiene in the bar.

Skills Required

Previous bar experience is essential, and in most cases a good working knowledge of the relevant language. Most importantly, however, employers will look for a lively and outgoing personality.

Minimum age ranges from 21 – 24, depending on responsibilities.

There are supervisory positions available - these will require previous bar management experience, a good level of numeracy, and fluent language skills.

Working Hours

Unless you work in a bar that only opens in the evening, it is likely that the job will involve a mixture of evening and day shifts. Evening shifts can often mean a very late finish, so chances of making the first lift on a regular basis are fairly slim!

You will normally work 6 days out of 7, with a full day off.

Package

Wages range from £60 - £100 week. Packages include food and accommodation, insurance, and return travel to the UK. With tour operators, lift passes and equipment hire will normally be included. Bars will not usually provide these, although wages are typically higher, and paid in local currency.

Tips are generally shared among the bar and/or waiting staff.

Pros & Cons

- ✔ Popularity ('friends' looking for freebies!)
- ✔ Free drinks
- ✔ Reasonable time on the mountain

- ✘ Drunk customers, whether they're mates or not!
- ✘ Long shifts
- ✘ Working unsociable hours

INSTRUCTOR

Duties, Hours, Package

Being an instructor has kudos. It means you're good and you ski or board for a living.

You will usually work 2/3 hours in the morning and afternoon, either in private lessons or with groups. One day off a week is the norm, except during school holidays.

The bonus is that at the end of the day your evenings are your own, but there will be times when you would much rather be in the off-piste with your friends than teaching another group of beginners.

The pay can vary considerably and often depends on how much work you do yourself. During school holidays everybody works, but in low season more experienced instructors may be the only ones with regular classes and/or private lessons.

Skills Required

Although working as an instructor may seem like a dream job, the reality is that in Europe at least it can be difficult to become sufficiently qualified to teach legally.

Whether right or wrong, for most European countries, but particularly in France, you cannot work legally without either having the local qualification or *equivalence* to that.

Non-BASI Qualification

It is easier to get a qualification to work in North America or New Zealand and there are a large number of good quality operations that will allow you to spend the winter in one of these locations, while qualifying for either the CSIA (Canada), PSIA (America) or NZSIA (New Zealand).

The drawback of these courses, apart from their cost, is that none of these qualifications will allow you to work in the main European resorts.

BASI Qualification

After a long political struggle, the British, French, Italian and Austrian governing bodies for skiing and snowboarding recently reached an agreement regarding the free movement of labour.

All of which rather grandly means that BASI (British Association of Snowsport Instructors) qualifications are recognised in Europe.

BASI 3 instructors can work in Europe, except in France, where BASI 2 instructors can work temporarily (up to three years) as *stagiares* or trainee, within certain approved training establishments.

In order to instruct fully in France, BASI-qualified instructors then have to complete either 'European Speed Test' or the BASI run 'UK Speed Test' within a certain time. This is a Giant Slalom race of a very high standard and only a small percentage qualifying each time.

The French System

An alternative is to become a *stagiare* via the French system by taking their qualification – the Test Technique. You will still have to pass the European Speed Test to qualify fully.

Pros & Cons

- ✔ Working outdoors all day
- ✔ Potential pulling power
- ✔ View from the office window!

- ✘ Lack of personal skiing time
- ✘ All day on the nursery slopes
- ✘ Constant exposure to elements can put years on you!

OFFICE JOBS

Most larger tour operators have an overseas office as well as a UK base, which opens up opportunities for skilled individuals.

The most common of these is office administrator or assistant, but there are a handful of positions available in specialist areas such as accountancy or IT.

Duties

As office administrator, you will provide support to the overseas management team, which can include communication with staff and suppliers, producing booking information and rooming lists for resorts, liaison with UK office, booking transfer coaches and co-ordinating transfer days, collating accounts, processing credit card payments and general office administration.

Accountants handle all overseas accounts, including reconciliation of resort accounts, controlling payment of suppliers, and preparation of financial reports.

IT positions vary, but can range from website maintenance to network support and systems control.

Skills Required

For admin positions, strong administrative and organisational skills are required, as well as excellent PC skills (Word, Excel). Knowledge of tour operator bookings systems such as FSS or JFA are also useful.

Either fluency, or a good working knowledge of the relevant language is required.

For accountancy positions, relevant qualifications are essential as is a good working knowledge or fluency in the relevant language.

IT positions can be very specific – relevant qualifications and experience are essential.

Working Hours

Don't despair – office jobs don't necessarily mean 9-5! Employers recognise the fact that you want some time on the slopes, and hours can be from around 8am to midday and then mid-afternoon until 7 or 8pm, offering a couple of hours on the mountain in the afternoon.

Most office jobs will offer one full day off per week.

Package

For an office administrator position, wages range from £100 - £150 week, and will usually include accommodation, lift pass, equipment, insurance, and return travel to the UK.

Where any of the benefits are not included, wages will be at the higher end of the scale.

For accounts positions, remuneration can vary dramatically, depending on previous experience, seniority of the position, and financial responsibilities – obviously the greater the responsibility, the higher the wages!

Similarly with IT positions, remuneration will depend on previous experience and the nature of the role, and will most likely be negotiable.

Where normal benefits are not included in the package, the salary will reflect this.

Career Opportunities

If you become hooked on seasons, there are genuine career opportunities for the right individuals, based in the UK and the Alps.

Positions include area manager, contracts manager, operations manager and various others, depending on the employer's overseas structure.

For all of these positions, either fluency or very good conversational skills in the relevant language is essential.

These roles carry lots of responsibility, and although you will be on the end of a mobile phone at all times, you have much less guest contact.

Senior positions tend to be year-round, meaning summer and winter spent in the mountains, with some of the autumn spent back in the UK.

Pros & Cons

- ✔ Regular working hours
- ✔ Full day off
- ✔ Reasonable time on the slopes

- ✘ Working in smaller team can be less sociable
- ✘ No guest contact
- ✘ Still a desk job!

Other Jobs

There are a variety of other positions in ski resorts, some of which require specialist qualifications and others that you may not have realised existed!

The following list is by no means exhaustive, but gives examples of some of the other jobs on offer.

Ski/Board Technician

Positions are available in hire shops and also with tour operators that provide their own equipment. Duties include ensuring clients' equipment needs are met, including fitting and maintenance of equipment, as well as controlling incoming and outgoing stock.

Relevant technician qualifications are required, and for most hire shops you will need to be proficient in the local language. Minimum age ranges from 18 – 21.

Masseur/Beautician

Some companies offer extra pampering to their guests, in the form of massage and beauty treatments, often in demand after a hard day on the slopes! Working hours tend to be during the morning and late afternoon/early evening, although some employers combine the role with hosting in a chalet.

Relevant qualifications and previous experience are required. Minimum age is usually 21.

Receptionist

Positions are available in either Club Hotels or in locally run hotels. Working hours will normally follow a shift pattern.

Fluency in the relevant language is essential, as well as an outgoing personality and excellent communication skills. Previous hotel reception experience is an advantage.

Driver

Many tour operators employ individuals to take on all driving duties in a resort. These can include driving guests to and from the slopes, taking children to ski school, deliveries of food, wine and laundry to chalets, driving staff to and from accommodation for work, and weekly food shopping.

Duties tend to be mainly in the mornings and late afternoon/early evening, or may be on a shift system. On transfer day, you may be required to drive guests to and from the airport.

A full, clean driving licence is required, as well as experience of driving overseas and/or larger vehicles. A few of the positions require you to hold a PCV licence.

Retail Jobs

In larger resorts, many of the shops require retail assistants for the sale of equipment and clothing. Fluency in the relevant language is required, as well as previous retail experience, and preferably some knowledge of technical equipment.

Working hours fall mostly during the day, but you will have one or two full days off and possibly some time off in the middle of the day.

DJ/Doorman

There are a few positions available for experienced DJs and doormen in nightclubs. Working hours are evenings only, with shifts finishing very late. Packages will consist of wages only, and are less likely to include accommodation and lift pass.

Where to Work

Two of the most common queries we receive at Natives are how to find jobs in Val d'Isère (usually in a bar) or in North America.

Certainly a season in both of these locations can be great fun, but anyone starting off with only these two options is limiting their chances right from the start.

Large or small?

The biggest misconception is that you have to be in a big resort to have a good season.

While a winter in Méribel or Val d'Isère offers a great ski area and choice of bars, there are so many Brits in these resorts that you will rarely if ever mix with the locals and by the end of the season there will still be hundreds of season workers that you have never even met.

A season in a smaller resort such as Châtel, La Rosière, Scheffau or Risoul may sound less appealing, but you will have a much stronger feeling of community with your fellow workers, all of whom you'll probably know.

You'll be more likely to improve your language skills and, crucially, away from the hordes, you'll be able to pick up fresh tracks days after snowfall. In the big resorts, the powder is often all chewed up by lunchtime the day after fresh snow.

Ultimately it is not possible to say that a season in one particular resort is better than any other. It will depend on so many factors - your colleagues, the snow, your employer, your chalet and most importantly, you.

Do you have a choice?

You can obviously restrict your job seeking to companies who only go to a particular resort, but taking an inflexible approach with a larger operator is unlikely to impress them.

If you really are keen on a resort, it is much more effective to make a company want to employ you first, while letting them know your preferred choice. Then the burden is on them to make an offer for the resort you're looking for.

Many companies do not finalise resort allocation until you complete the training course.

In most cases you will have already been pencilled in for a particular resort and/or chalet, but they will want to assess if you're the right person to work on your own or with the rest of the team around you.

Where to Work

Which Country?

France is the most popular country with British skiers and boarders (37% of all holidaymakers), followed by Austria (19%), Italy (15%), Andorra (13%) and Switzerland (7%), with only 6% heading across the pond to North America.

However because the British market is based on chalet holidays - 46% stay in chalets or club hotels - the number of jobs available is even more biased towards the traditional Alpine countries of Europe.

It is estimated that up to 40% of all British workers are based in France alone, principally located in the large resorts of the Tarentaise.

Working in North America

Despite the fact that there are very few jobs available with British tour operators in North America, we are constantly asked about how to find a job over there!

Unfortunately it is highly unlikely you will be able to find work legally in the States or Canada unless you can obtain a visa through BUNAC or have done seasons before with a British tour operator and get transferred there from the European programme.

Full details of this are covered in our Visa section on page 33.

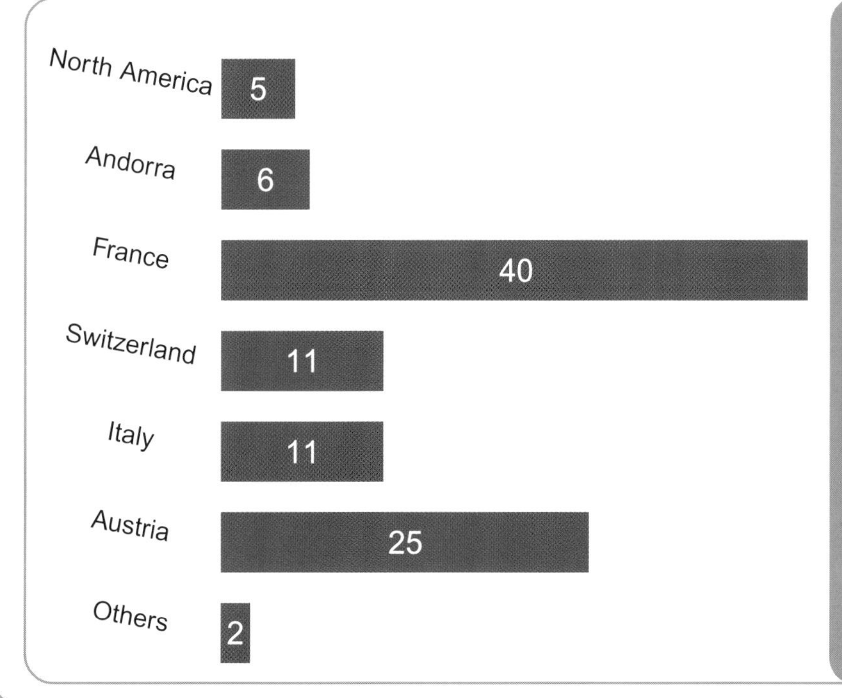

The ten resorts with the most British staff

1. Val d'Isère
2. Méribel
3. Courchevel
4. La Plagne
5. Alpe d'Huez
6. Les Deux Alpes
7. St Anton
8. Kitzbühel
9. Verbier
10. Chamonix

What's in it for me?

You may have read through the job descriptions over the past few pages and thought that it sounds like a lot of hard work for not much money.

Well, you're right and wrong…

Hard work

There's no point denying it – working a ski season is hard work.

The working week can be anything from 40 to 80 hours (if you're resort manager or a senior rep), and in many cases you are effectively on call at all times. It's just one day off a week and resort managers may not even manage that.

If you are not prepared to work hard, you might as well stop looking for a job now.

Make friends for life

When you work and live in such a close environment as a ski resort, you end up spending a lot of time together.

And the great part about working a season is that so much of it is quality time – sunshine, powder, smiles.

When you work a ski season you make friends for life – how do you put a value on that?

Be a hot skier/boarder

Whether you start the season as a beginner or advanced, you will finish the season significantly better. (Unless of course you become a fair-weather skier, as some snow bunnies are inclined to do.)

Career potential

Around 30% of all staff go back for another season. That's why Natives exists - because working a season is addictive.

Plenty of returners eventually end up working for ski companies or elsewhere in the travel industry, working in product, marketing, contracting, HR and sales.

Improve your languages

Unless you head to one of the smaller resorts, it is surprisingly hard to use your language skills. In places like Méribel and Val d'Isère many of your suppliers will be British and those who aren't are often fluent in English.

Despite this, there will plenty of opportunities if you want to make the effort to learn the language, particularly for reps, who can make small talk with the coach driver during long transfers to the airport (although in reality you will probably want to sleep instead).

Experience life…

Have you ever seen an avalanche? A full moon rise over white mountains? Ever ridden off-piste so light and deep you need a snorkel? Parapented? Been on a skidoo? Watched a sunrise in the Alps (you'll see plenty of these on transfer days)? Maybe just watched it snow, with fat snowflakes piling up on your windowsill?

We could go on, but hopefully you get the point.

ONLY £50 PER WEEK???

It is true that some jobs can pay as little as £50 per week. Hopefully we've established on the opposite page that you can get much more out of a season than you can ever value in monetary terms. However, you should bear in mind that the financial side of things can be better than it looks.

Package

Don't forget that the travel, accommodation, lift pass, ski equipment, insurance and food your employer provides is probably worth about £3500 across the season.

In fact once you are out there, how you spend your money often comes down to vices - drinking, smoking and shopping!

And even if you do have a few vices, it can still be possible to come home at the end of the season with a decent amount of savings, made from less than five months' work.

Tips

For chalet staff, this is likely to be your main source of extra income. Not all your guests tip and you certainly can't pick those who will. The best advice is to put your head down, do the work and be yourself. Strangely, the best chalet staff usually get the best tips...

Cheap Drinks

Depending on your resort you will usually also get a reduced rate or free drinks from the local bars. In big resorts you might save 25% a drink, but in smaller, cosy resorts you may not need to put your hand in your pocket all season.

Local Discounts

Look after your suppliers and they will look after you. Cakes, leftovers and flirting can keep your hire shop staff in good spirits and ensure a big discount when you come to buy the board or that ski jacket you've had your eye on.

Packed Lunches

With lunch on the mountain a costly affair, budget conscious Brits can be easily tempted by a good-value packed lunch. A doorstop sandwich, a fun-size bar and piece of fruit for a few quid can turn into a great earner. You should however check with your employer for their policy on this.

Mini-bar

Whether you can get away with buying beers for 10p at your local hypermarché and selling them at a healthy profit will depend on what country you are in and what company you work for. Selling alcohol without a licence is illegal in most countries, but mixers for duty free can still return a decent profit.

Internet Access

If you've got your own laptop, then you could offer a mini-Internet service by undercutting local Internet cafes.

Other Ideas

Staff can earn money selling books, guides, videos, sweatshirts, T-shirts, hats, paintings and almost everything else. We recommend you are selective and don't prostitute yourself (although if you really want to earn money…!).

Dodgy Dealing

Some staff try to scam their employers with variations on what is, in effect, theft. We do not suggest you engage in anything like this. If you are caught you face instant dismissal, with possible legal repercussions.

getting the job

Now that you know the different positions that are on offer, you probably have an idea of the job you'd like or would be most suitable for, and can start making progress towards getting it.

The actual process of securing a position can be lengthy, and it may seem like you're investing a lot of time at this stage with little reward, but with enthusiasm and effort, it'll pay off in the end.

You need to begin by getting your CV into shape and completing the necessary application forms, possibly building on your skills by attending a course, and hopefully as a result, attending some interviews.

The following chapter will guide you through this stage, offering a wealth of insider information on when and how to apply, on specialist courses and visa restrictions, as well as advice on preparing your CV, completing application forms, and interview tips.

Try to keep an open mind at this stage with regards to the positions you'll take, and your choice of resort - you can always be choosy at a later stage when you receive a stack of job offers!

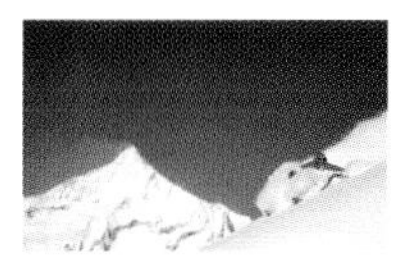

When to Apply

The main recruitment period is July to October, although some companies do begin advertising earlier. During this peak time, tour operators are continually reviewing application forms and CVs, and interviewing candidates.

Travelling

If you plan to travel or work overseas during this period, bear in mind that employers will want you to attend an interview, therefore it will be difficult to get the ball rolling until you return to the UK.

Last Minute Jobs

Don't panic if you haven't secured a job by November. There are still jobs available at the last minute and companies regularly contact Natives up to the beginning of the season due to staff dropping out.

However, most of these jobs are for skilled and qualified staff, so please remember that the later you leave it, the less choice you'll have.

During the Season

If you do miss the start for any reason, there are still some jobs available during the season, due to the inevitable staff turnover.

Contrary to popular belief, working a ski season is quite hard work and the combination of long hours, late nights and strenuous activity is something that not everyone can cope with.

There are often a number of resignations and departures due to injury in the first couple of weeks in January, so this is a good time to apply if you decide you want to work the remainder of the season.

Again most of these are for skilled staff, with jobs mainly for nannies, chefs, chalet staff and some positions for reps.

It is quite possible for the right person to be interviewed over the phone one day and flown out the next, so if you are looking for something after the season has started, it will be to your advantage if you are available and ready to leave at short notice!

Positions crop up from time to time throughout January and February, but by the beginning of March, employers usually cope until the end of the season with the staff they have.

How to Apply

The application process can be time consuming, as well as disheartening - it's important to stay positive and remember that perseverance will pay off!

The following are ways in which you can apply:

Online - Natives.co.uk

Natives is the leading supplier of winter staff in the UK. Hundreds of employers have used our services, and during the peak recruitment period there can be over 500 positions advertised, all of which can be applied for online.

If you don't find what you're looking for at first, don't forget you can just give us a call and we will point you in the right direction.

Offline - Direct

An alternative to applying online is to ring round or write to the companies direct, asking for an application form to be sent out. You can also try approaching companies about jobs at the Ski Shows, although this is less effective than it used to be.

Letters on spec to larger companies rarely produce more than an application form, although smaller companies are more likely to respond positively.

Finding work in resort

We do not recommend heading out to resort and then trying to find a job, as it has a very low success rate.

You will need accommodation and enough cash to support yourself until you find something, and many people return home empty handed after a couple of frustrating weeks of door knocking.

If you do decide to try this method, ensure you have lots of copies of your CV, talk to as many staff in resort as possible and find out the phone numbers of all the resort reps and managers, so that they know you're available and can contact you if they need staff in a hurry!

Application Forms

These can be time consuming, but are worth spending the time on, as they can make the difference between being offered an interview or not. Employers receive thousands of application forms, which are scanned very quickly, so it is vital that yours makes the grade!

The following basic guidelines should help you:

- If it is a hard copy, always write in black ink – forms are often photocopied several times.

- Always write neatly and legibly – prepare lengthy responses first on rough paper, until you're happy that it reads well - then check for spelling errors before transferring onto the actual form.

- Ensure all contact details are included, and entered correctly – it is irritating for all concerned if a good candidate misses out because one digit of their phone number is incorrect.

- Complete all relevant fields and questions.

- Use areas in which you can sell yourself wisely – for example if asked what you can offer the company, don't just write one sentence – this is your chance to shine!

- Don't over-enthuse about wanting to ski/board as much as possible – although employers recognise that this is the main reason for working in a ski resort, they want to be sure that first and foremost you will be committed to the position they're interviewing you for.

- Never lie about your abilities – you will always be caught out at some stage, most likely on the training course in front of your new mates!

- Where requested, attach a photograph – this should be a passport style photo, avoid the 'mug shot' style and SMILE!

CVs

A strong CV makes a huge difference in securing a job, so is worth investing time on – employers may spend only 10-20 seconds scanning each CV, so it is vital that yours stands out for the right reasons!

General Tips

Try to fit onto 2 pages if possible. Employers don't want to wade through several sheets of A4 even if you do have extensive experience – keep it concise.

Check and re-check for spelling mistakes and typos, then ask a friend or a relative to double check it.

Be honest – there is absolutely no point in lying about your skills and experience – you will only look like a fool at a later stage.

Contact Details

Generally these should be at the top of your CV - ensure these are all up to date. Date of birth and nationality should also be included in this section.

Profile

This section is optional, but can be a great way of stating goals, and summarising key skills and attributes in one paragraph.

Employment History

Always list the most recent first, and work backwards. Rather than just listing duties and responsibilities for each role, highlight achievements made, for example 'increased overall customer satisfaction from 70% to 98%'. Bullet points are more effective than long-winded paragraphs.

If you have had lots of jobs, don't include less relevant ones, for example working in a factory during university holidays. On the other hand, if you are a school leaver without much work experience, include everything.

It is not usually necessary to include details of why you are no longer working in each job listed.

Qualifications

Again, these should be listed most recent first, working backwards – only list subjects and grades for higher qualifications.

Skills and Achievements

In this section you can list additional skills, for example languages, PC skills, driving licence details, cookery courses and other certificates and awards that may be relevant.

Interests

This section is less important, but should always be included, as your interests give the employer more of an insight into your personality, and the information can often be used as an icebreaker in an interview.

References

If you do list referees, ensure their contact details are up to date. Otherwise, you can state 'references available on request'.

Tailoring your CV

CVs should always be tailored to the position you are applying for, placing more emphasis on the skills and experience relevant to that role.

For example, if applying for a resort rep position, you should focus on previous customer service experience, as well as organisation skills, language skills and skiing/boarding ability.

Some of your experience may not seem relevant to a ski season, but within your work experience any potential employer will see evidence of key skills such as communication, organisational and social skills, all of which are very important for seasonal positions.

Classic Mistakes...

“Suspected to graduate early next year”
“Proven ability to track down and correct erors."
"Here are my qualifications for you to overlook"
"Am a perfectionist and rarely if if ever forget details"
“I have an excellent track record, although I am not a horse"

Menu Plans

When applying for chalet positions, you will usually be asked to submit a 6-day menu plan.

As with CVs and application forms, this is worth spending time on, as it will make a significant difference in securing an interview.

The menu plan should include 6 evening meals, each consisting of a starter, main meal, vegetarian main, and dessert. You can also include canapés, and a selection of cakes and biscuits that you might serve for afternoon tea.

What not to include!

- Stews and casseroles are generally not acceptable, although boeuf bourgignonne may pass, and is great for a changeover day
- Desserts should always be prepared from scratch or cooked
- Avoid too many chocolate based or very rich desserts - try to alternate with lighter, fruity desserts
- Pasta as a main dish is generally not acceptable, unless incorporated into a theme night, when it will be necessary to provide a variety of dishes on that theme
- Avoid curry or highly spiced dishes as people tend to either love or hate spicy food. Also, ingredients for such dishes may be unavailable or costly in many resorts
- Any dishes containing minced beef should be avoided, for example chilli or spaghetti bolognaise, as this is seen as 'budget' food

Most companies will require you to work to a budget, but do not worry about this at application stage – you should aim to make your menu plan as creative as possible so that it stands out.

The following basic guidelines should be considered when putting together your menu plan:

Cooking Ability

It's pointless pulling dishes straight out of recipe books that you have no idea how to cook.

Only include dishes on your menu that you have cooked before - if not, you will only look foolish later, either at interview stage, or even worse, in resort!

Main Dishes

These should always consist of a meat or fish dish, accompanied by a carbohydrate, usually potatoes (there are many different ways of cooking and presenting potatoes to avoid repetition), rice or pasta and two types of vegetable (not just boiled veg!) cooked and presented creatively.

Combinations

When putting dishes together, take into account both taste and presentation – try to visualise the dish on a plate, and think about the combination of colours and flavours.

Variety

Ensure you vary the main ingredient between the starter and main course, for example, if goat's cheese is the starter, then avoid chicken stuffed with brie for the main course. Similarly, if the main meal is quite heavy, you should choose a lighter dessert.

Vegetarians

Many people struggle with ideas for vegetarian meals, but efforts must be made to ensure that they are as tasty and varied as meat dishes. Vegetarian guests have paid just as much for their holidays, and will expect the same standard.

Try and avoid the common mistake of serving too many egg/cheese dishes.

Descriptions

The language used to describe the dishes on your menu can also make a difference.

For example a simple salad sounds a lot more interesting when described as "tomato and mozzarella salad, served on a bed of fresh basil leaves, drizzled with balsamic vinegar.'

Layout

When drawing up a menu, you can either put the dishes in a table format, or lay it out like a restaurant menu

Day 1

Honey Mustard dressed Goat's Cheese Salad

Pork Escalope with Mushroom and Spinach sauce

Hassleback potatoes and balsamic roasted vegetables

V Aubergine Escalope with Mushroom and Spinach sauce

Individual Fruit Crumbles served with ice cream

COURSES

Whatever ski season job you are looking for, there are a number of ways to increase your chances of landing the position you're after...

Cookery Courses

If you'd like to run a chalet, but aren't confident that your cooking skills are up to the required standard, then a cookery course will not only increase your skills and knowledge, but will also significantly increase your chances of securing a job.

There are a variety of cookery courses available, both in the UK and overseas. Unfortunately few of these are specialist chalet courses, and can often be punitively expensive.

As a result, three years ago, Natives developed our own intensive chalet cookery course, now recognised throughout the industry by all the main tour operators as well as smaller, private chalet companies.

Our five-day course is not only cheap er than most alternatives - it is the only one to be run entirely by current season workers and to include specialist seasonal knowledge as well as the required cooking skills.

When and where?

Courses take place mainly in July and August, with a later course in October.

The current location of the course is St Teresa's School for Girls, in its picturesque surroundings at Effingham, Surrey.

What will I learn?

The course contains a mixture of practical and theory sessions, offering specialist knowledge that will help you to run a chalet efficiently as well as improve your cooking skills.

Main Course Sessions

These start with a demonstration followed by a practical session in which students work in pairs on different recipes. Course tutors give on-the-job coaching during the practical session.

Students and tutors then try the different meals and discuss the challenges they came across in the preparation of each recipe.

Specialist Sessions

These shorter specialist sessions focus on key elements that all good cooks need to know, plus some chalet specific information:

- Cakes
- Vegetables
- Children's Meals
- Starters
- Special Diets
- Desserts
- Soups
- Canapés

Knowledge Sessions

These focus on those particular elements of running a chalet that are essential preparation and information for staff. These include:

- Safety and Hygiene in the Kitchen
- Menu Planning and Presentation
- Time Saving and Budget Saving Tips
- Accounting/Budgeting
- Shopping
- Guest Management

Courses are limited to 12 places, with two tutors, meaning you can gain maximum benefit from the personal attention.

Candidates are assessed throughout the course, and are given continuous feedback on performance, so that strengths can be utilised, and areas of weakness improved on.

Booking & More Info

Demand for our courses is usually very high. Places begin to fill up early in the year and courses are usually full by June.

For more information, or to secure a place on one of the courses, call us on 08700 463377 or take a look at www.natives.co.uk/skijobs/cookery

55 £50.00

COURSES

Job Workshops

During the summer months, Natives run a series of Job Workshops, designed to offer useful advice and information to anyone looking to work in a ski resort.

These two hour sessions will benefit most job seekers, whether at the very beginning of the application process and unsure of quite where to start, or with interviews lined up, and wanting advice on interview technique, or tips on choosing which position to accept.

If you have read through this Guide, but would prefer to be able to have someone answer your questions in person, then the Natives Job Workshop could be for you.

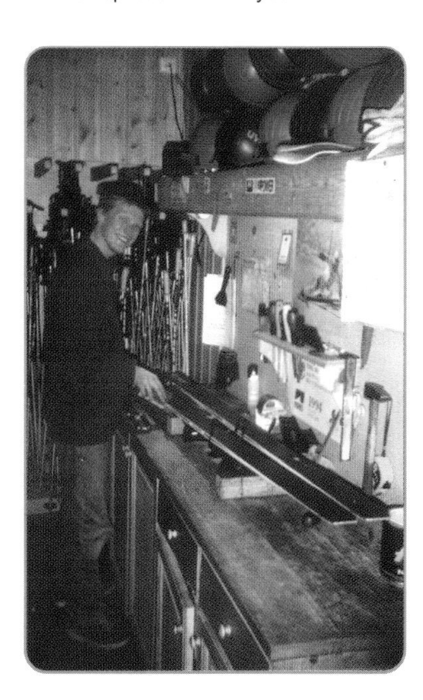

Featured Topics

- Main jobs available and skills required
- Package and possible 'extras'
- How to handle the application form
- Advice on preparing your CV
- Interview advice and tips
- Questions you should be asking potential employers

Location and Timings

Sessions are held at Natives' head office in Putney, South-West London and occasionally regionally around the UK.

For more information, check out www.natives.co.uk/skijobs/workshops or call 08700 463377.

Ski Tech Courses

Another great way to work a season in the Alps, or even to get into the industry in the UK, is to work as a Ski or Snowboard Technician.

In conjunction with the industry specialists, Anything Technical, Natives offers a number of fully certified courses, all recognised by the main UK retailers and overseas employers.

All courses are designed to give hands-on experience, and wherever possible are limited to 12 people per day.

There are three day courses available:

- Ski/Snowboard Technican Course (Beginners)
- Ski/Snowboard Technician Course (Advanced)
- Boot Fitting Seminar

Locations

Courses are held in the Anything Technical workshop in Kendal, Cumbria and in the UK offices of Salomon in Basingstoke, Hants. Both are among the most sophisticated workshops in the UK with state of the art machinery.

Booking

To book a place or for more info check www.natives.co.uk/skijobs/skitech

INTERVIEWS

For most jobs you will have to attend an interview. Not many people enjoy interviews, but the following guidelines should help you on your way…

Punctuality

Ensure you arrive on time by knowing exactly where you are going and how to get there. Always allow for delays.

Aim to arrive early – usually you will be able to find a café in which to kill some time and collect your thoughts. If you are unavoidably delayed, always ring to let the employer know.

Research

Before the interview, always make an effort to find out about the company from their brochure or website. Find out what market they target, whether they specialise in a particular country, and any useful statistics such as their percentage of returning guests.

Find out as much as possible about the job you are applying for – most companies will include job descriptions in their application pack, and often on their website.

You should also establish the format of the interview, for example whether it will be a group assessment or individual interview. Is there is anything specific you need to bring with you?

Preparation

Just as the employer is trying to establish whether you are right for the job, the interview is also your chance to find out whether the job is right for you. Prepare some questions and practice asking them before the interview.

Most employers will run through the package on offer. Good questions can be about how many people you are likely to be sharing with, location of staff accommodation, whether the lift pass is a full area pass, and whether you will eat with guests.

Common Questions

You will almost always be asked about your strengths and weaknesses. With weaknesses, try to identify one that is easily remedied, as you will probably be asked how you would overcome this.

Be prepared to talk about your achievements – you will usually be asked for specific examples of achievements you feel proud of, or examples of how you've overcome difficult situations.

Focus

Avoid rambling – keep it relevant – and talking too much. The ability to listen is extremely important, and employers will be noting your communication skills throughout the interview.

Be Positive

Always be positive about past experiences. If you are unable to avoid talking about negative points, ensure that you show you've taken something positive from it.

Never criticise previous employers – this is extremely unprofessional, and will always put off potential employers.

First Impressions

'You never get a second chance to make a first impression'. Always dress smartly in simple business attire, offer a firm handshake, a winning smile, and maintain good eye contact throughout.

Persevere

Don't be disheartened if you are not offered a job every time – we all have bad days, and chances are that if you're turned down, perhaps the job or company wasn't for you.

Don't forget that your interview technique will improve with the number of interviews you attend, so it's all good experience.

VISAS

Unfortunately, visa and passport restrictions often mean that you will not be able to work in certain countries. So, before you begin dreaming of that perfect job in the perfect place (eg North America) you should check the legal situation.

The following guidelines are subject to change and are certainly not definitive. If you are in any doubt about whether you will be working legally, it is always best to check with your potential employer and/or the appropriate embassy.

EU

For positions in the EU (eg France, Austria, Italy), most British tour operators require employees to hold an EU passport.

In some cases smaller, independent operators may only require a valid UK working visa for the period of employment, in conjunction with a UK National Insurance number.

Ancestry Visas, Right of Abode, and UK Working Visas do not count as an EU passport.

Non-EU countries

Most of these countries retain a degree of flexibility, but if you are working in Switzerland for the season, you will require a work permit.

Employers generally obtain these on your behalf, but make sure you have a valid one for your whole period of employment, as resorts are inspected regularly during the season, and anyone found working illegally can be deported.

USA/Canada

One of the most common questions we are asked at Natives is how to go about working a season in the States or in Canada.

Unfortunately, visa restrictions make this quite difficult. Either a working visa or a US/Canadian passport is required in order to work legally, and the reality is that it is very difficult to obtain a work visa without a job offer, and vice-versa.

Exceptions

British tour operators commonly have to purchase work visas on behalf of their staff. Consequently they often place good quality returning staff who they know they can rely on (and will not have to replace at great expense!) in positions in North America.

It's a longer route, but why not try a season in Europe first, and make sure you make a good impression!

Alternatively, if you are aged between 18 and 29, and are currently a full-time student, or a gap year student with an unconditional course offer, then you may be eligible for a working visa through BUNAC's Work America or Work Canada programme.

See the BUNAC website at www.bunac.org for further details.

We then either approach British tour operators on your behalf or you can head out to resort and pick up a job legally on the spot.

New Zealand/Australia

The outlook is far more positive for working a season in the Southern Hemisphere. Although a working visa is required, these are easier to obtain.

If you are a UK national aged 18 – 30, you can apply for a working holiday visa through the relevant embassy, which is intended to allow you to work in order to fund your travels.

The procedure is relatively straightforward, but whether you obtain a visa depends on how many are left from the annual allocation when you apply. Currently the New Zealand annual allocation is renewed on the 1st September.

Further information about obtaining the visa can be found on the relevant embassy websites:
www.nzembassy.com
www.australia.org.uk

not working

To the uninformed, doing a ski season in any shape or form is good enough to label you a ski bum.

But among *saisonniers* themselves, the ski bum is quite definitely a different breed from workers.

If you're a ski bum, then by definition you don't work. And if you do work, you certainly don't work for a tour operator and have guests to deal with.

You might take on some ad-hoc employment, like cleaning apartments, shovelling snow, or washing up for the local bar in lieu of beer, but this is usually a one-off.

Work rarely bothers the ski bum, who can lie in when the weather's bad, or first lift when it's perfect powder. Being a ski bum means freedom.

Unfortunately it also means that without a decent amount of money behind you, it can often mean freedom from the comforts of life as well.

The wages might not be great working for a tour op, but add in the cost of your accommodation, food, lift pass and all the other benefits like free chalet wine, then from the outside it can soon look like a life of luxury.

Despite this each season more and more people choose not to work and to join the ski bum trail. We look at the pros and cons, because let's face it - who really, honestly, wants to work during their season?

Surviving as a Ski Bum

Be lucky

Rock up at the start of the season and get a cheap deal on a great flat in the centre of resort.

Alternatively, meet a wealthy chalet owner and get paid to house-sit while he's not there (amazingly this has happened). Make good use of his top of the range 4x4 (you need to keep cars running or they freeze up, right?) and become the most popular bum in town.

Befriend the chalet staff

Make friends with all the chalet girls/boys (helps if you have that irresistible cheeky face and naughty twinkle in your eye).

Flirt outrageously, while never exercising favouritism and you will have the perfect balance of unlimited free food and sex. Easy.

Befriend the bar staff

Make good friends with bar owners/staff and get all your drinks for free. In return, entertain them with your great wit and impressive tales of mountain madness.

Occasionally help out by DJing/doing promotions on special nights, in return for more free drinks.

Have a face that fits

Happen to look exactly like the first worker to be sent home with an injury and 'borrow' their season lift pass.

Alternatively, make friends with a ski instructor/pisteur, who lets you have his/her old uniform so you don't even need to bother with queuing for lifts (seriously, we've seen this happen).

Coin it...

Offer your services around resort as freelance bar person / photographer / driver and negotiate lucrative contracts to fit in with your hectic schedule of boarding/skiing, partying and sleeping.

Alternatively, get spotted by a Salomon/Burton scout who spies your potential and pays you to live the life. End up coming home with more money that you started with.

TOP TIP - Sort your accommodation early doors

Natives helps arrange accommodation for lots of *saisonniers* every season. Working with our seasonal lets partner, PlanetSubZero, we have a wide range of apartments available in all sizes and resorts.

Options are available for couples, groups, or individuals – with shared apartments or PlanetSubZero's own properties in Tignes, Les Arcs and Chamonix.

Bear in mind that for a decent amount of living space, you can expect to pay a minimum of £2000 (Chamonix) to £2500 (Val d'Isère). Cramming people in can bring the price down, but 'what you pay for is what you get' has never rung more true!

Full details of our seasonal lets service are available at www.natives.co.uk/travel/lets

Reality Bites

OK – the previous page may be far fetched, but it can happen. The sad truth is that for every successful season bummed, there's many more who've failed miserably in their quest for ultimate snow nirvana.

Nowhere to live

Rock up only to find that you're 6 months too late and all the accommodation went in August. Beg and plead a space on someone's floor for a few nights.

Be grateful for your sleeping bag and try not to listen to your kind host 'entertaining' their latest conquest three inches from your head.

Get kicked out on Christmas Eve, after you're caught with your tongue 'accidentally' down said conquest's throat, forcing you to blow half your budget paying tourist rates for a bed over Christmas and New Year. Go home at the end of January when your money runs out.

Nothing to eat

Discover that most new chalet staff 'can't cook, won't cook' and spend a fortune on burgers to stave off imminent starvation.

Spend your first few weeks feeling too cold, hungry, hungover and tired to go up the mountain. Contract flu as a result of poor living conditions and spend £50 on antibiotics. Remember you forgot about travel insurance.

Spend all your money

Show your commitment to friendship with (the bank of) bar owners by investing all your money with them. Entertain them with drunken antics and your best party tricks, only to have them laugh in your face when you ask about possible jobs. 'Reshposhible, moi?! Coursh I am.'

Blame beer monster for lack of notes in your wallet and report the theft to the police. Ring home for emergency funds.

Have a face that fits (but not know it)

Spend £400 on your season lift pass, only to find out two days later that the guy/girl who looked exactly like you has broken his leg and is going home. Try (and fail) to resell your lift pass to the lift pass office.

Earn a crust (literally)

Offer your services around resort as freelance bar person / photographer / driver.

After three weeks of 'Je cherche du travail', feel lucky when you're offered a trial day's pot washing at £2/hour. Cherish the £10 you've made for 5 hours work, and do not resent the fact that you were scrubbing cheese (aka cement) off saucepans while all your mates were out enjoying the first big dump of the season.

OK - exaggerated perhaps, but not so far from reality. Bumming a season is fun but hard work, and by no means guaranteed to succeed.

before you go

The easy part was getting the job. Now you've got to deal with the wait until the season starts.

This can seem like an eternity, as you wait for the day to arrive when you head off. Fortunately, Natives is with you all the way in the long lead-up to the season.

It starts in **August** when the first ski and board mags come out and you find yourself visiting WHSmith every day waiting for them to hit the shelves.

By **September** the first trade shows come around touring Southampton, Birmingham and Manchester through **October**, climaxing with Daily Mail Ski Show and Board-X in London.

We run loads of promotions through the autumn, giving away free and discounted tickets to all the shows, movie premieres and pretty much every snowsports event going.

These all run through to the Natives Workers Party on the first Saturday in November, which marks the start of our Show Love Tour and (Pete Tong voice please) 'The Official Start to the Season'.

Into **November**, our Chat Room gets hyper, and you'll find yourself checking the webcams and snow reports on a daily basis, until suddenly the time has come and you're on your way.

When you're not online, there are a few chores still to be done. The next few pages give you some tips on what to watch out for before you go.

What to take with you

Will your favourite teddy make the cut? The Burberry PJs? Your Becks/J-Lo poster?

Unless you're travelling out in your own car, your luggage allowance will be strictly limited by either airline or employer, so here's some tips on what to take with you for your season.

Skis/Boards/Boots
For most jobs you'll be on a deal where you get free equipment from the local hire shop.

This is great for beginners, but not so for experienced skiers/boarders, who are unlikely to get anything decent until the shop workers get to know you (or you bribe them with cakes). Experienced riders should take their own boards, while checking their insurance details carefully (snow-boards are the most commonly stolen item in ski resorts).

The options are better for skiers. Some workers take their own skis, plus the free pair from the shop. This way if the conditions are ropey at the start of the season you don't need to worry (as much) about trashing the bases and you can get them serviced for free.
In all cases, if you have your own boots, take them. Hire boots are rarely comfy.

Alarm Clock
Essential – if you don't wake easily try for the most irritating wake-up call possible. If you don't get up in the morning, you'll soon have nothing to get up for (not as good as it sounds!).

Take a Magimix
A sneaky way of getting past your employer's baggage allowance. A Magimix (food processor) is far too useful to be turned away, so fill the box with the CDs and stuff you couldn't fit in your other bags.

Condoms
Usually straightforward to get hold of in the mountains, if difficult to buy on your budget. We recommend you take your own supply unless you want the local pharmacist (wife of your hire shop owner/sister of your chalet owner) tracking your libido.

Pencil-case
Great for keeping your budget money in. A calculator is also useful.

Music
You will get bored of all your music. Take as many CDs as possible, squeezing extras in the Magimix box.

Visitors' Book
If you're running a chalet it's a great idea to have somewhere for your guests to write their comments. Your visitors' book will fill with lift-pass photos, poems, paeans to your cooking and remind you of the great times (and possibly some bad ones) you had with your guests.

Laptop/PC
Okay, so not within everyone's budget, but will make your accounts easier and you can still collect your Natives emails and Show Love Tour invites. The more entrepreneurial might consider offering an Internet access service.

Other Ideas
Thermals are not usually necessary with modern technical clothing. Swimming togs are an option for bad weather days. Lots of fancy dress parties mean you will probably have the opportunity to wear all of the following during a season (if so inclined): school uniform, wigs, gimp suit, DJ, wetsuit etc.

The Obvious

- **Gloves** – make sure they're waterproof, adjustable and warm
- **Sunnies** – no market stall savings here, protect your eyes!
- **Pants/salopettes** – must be waterproof, a padded bum is also useful for beginners
- **Jacket** – you won't want to ski in your company uniform
- **Hat** – avoid jester hats, which are big, but not clever
- **Ski socks** – for the sake of others, please take at least three pairs
- **Suncream** – very expensive in resort
- **Camera** – for memories of fantastic days and fantastic people
- **Boots** – take Timberlands, your trainers won't look so cool on ice!

FITNESS

Get Fit

As the main reason you're probably heading to the snow is to go skiing or boarding, it's worth investing some time getting prepared for the physical demands of a season.

Training

Start training at least 6 weeks before you head out. Everyone has their own preferred forms of exercise, but there are three areas you need to think about with skiing and boarding:

- **Aerobic fitness** - General fitness, gained from exercise which raises your heart rate and keeps it there over 20 minutes or more.

- **Anaerobic fitness** – Strength and the ability to sustain short bursts of exertion. Off-piste and freeriding both require real power and stamina.

- **Balance and flexibility** – To give you a more dynamic range of movement.

Cycling is a great option, as it can improve strength, stamina, anticipation and balance all in one go. Don't forget as well the great selection of dry and snow slopes around the UK, where you can get some real practice in before you go.

Check www.natives.co.uk/dryski.htm for your nearest slope.

Stay Fit

You should not underestimate how taxing December will be.

The trials and tribulations of setting up resort, dealing with your first guests, partying non-stop and spending your time on the mountain will take it out of you big time.

Living and working in the close proximity of a ski resort means that 'bugs' often move very fast through such a small community. By January, many resort staff end up picking up colds, flu and coughs that can take weeks to shake off.

Viruses and colds strike when you're run down so the best advice we can offer is to pace yourself, with the odd night in. Keep up your intake of fruit and veg, drink lots of water and stay away from the crèche (and nannies!).

Altitude Sickness

If you're working out in the Rockies, living above 2500m, you may find you initially have trouble sleeping, headaches and nausea.

Don't worry about this, as your body will soon adjust, but do take it easy for the first few days, watching your alcohol intake and drinking plenty of water

Hangovers

Although the clean air and water of the Alps makes hangovers less common, the vast quantity of alcohol that gets knocked back guarantees you'll have at least a few hangovers during a season.

Avoiding too much and too many different forms of booze is the simplest solution. Failing that you should be wary of chalet wine, which can be decidedly ropey in any quantity, and most definitely steer clear of Mutzig, a cloudy French lager that sneaks up on you with a large mallet and gives you no mercy.

If you can't avoid drinking, one sure way to reduce the likelihood of a hangover is to drink plenty of water before going to bed. The extra fluid helps reduce the dehydrating effects of alcohol and speeds up the elimination of toxins from the body.

Safety Tips

- Always warm up first
- Don't mix alcohol and riding
- Go fast, but stay in control
- Do that 'one last run' tomorrow

INSURANCE

Whether going for a season or a week, if you're on the mountain - you must have insurance. The alternative (including blood wagon, helicopters, pisteurs, ambulances and hospital) is the risk of a very big bill.

If you're employed by a tour operator, your package will usually include insurance cover for the season.

You should check the policy in detail before you go. From a medical point of view you should be okay in the case of any major accidents, but if your policy has an excess of say £30 on medical claims, any visit to the doctor (almost inevitable at some point) will end up costing you a significant proportion of your weekly wage.

Equipment Cover

In terms of equipment, you should again check the excess and maximum amount you can claim. If you break or have your equipment stolen you may well end up with very little back relying solely on your employer's cover.

Specialist Activities

It's also worth checking whether high risk activities such as off-piste, racing and parapenting are included. You're bound to want to do these at some point during the season, so it's worth taking into account.

A way round this in France is to buy a 'Carte Neige' or 'Carre Neige' that will cover you for off-piste skiing/boarding. Bear in mind though that a Carte Neige does not usually cover repatriation to the UK, nor some associated hospital costs.

E111

UK nationals should definitely ensure they have an E111 form, which can be picked up at any Post Office. Some employers have now made this compulsory for staff.

This allows you to take advantage of the reciprocal health agreements that Britain has with 40 countries over the world (does not include Canada and the USA). However, the E111 will not cover you for all treatment, nor blood-wagon or ambulance journeys.

Season Insurance Policies

In some cases it may be worthwhile investing in an additional policy of your own.

Check www.season-insurance.co.uk for policies recommended by Natives, available from £129 for the season.

Avalanche Safety

If you're heading out to work a season the chances are that at some point you'll explore the area and take in some of the off-piste.

The golden rule of backcountry to remember is to AVOID avalanches. Everyone should be properly equipped and trained to deal with an avalanche but nobody should ever have to!

1. History

Take into account the overall situation. When did it last snow? Has it been warm or cold? How windy has it been? Have there been many avalanches on this slope before?

There is no substitute for local knowledge – something you are unlikely to have after only a few weeks in resort.

2. Slope selection

How steep is it?
Below 25 degrees is not steep enough to slide, above 50 degrees is too steep to hold a lot of snow, anywhere between is prime avalanche territory.

Is the slope concave or convex?
Convex slopes do not support the weight of the snow high up very well and are more prone to avalanche.

What is the slope's aspect?
North-facing slopes are less affected by the sun and colder just after it has snowed. This is especially true in the springtime where north-facing slopes can remain dangerous for days or weeks after a snowfall.

Is the snow wind affected?
If the wind has been from behind it will

have deposited a lot of snow on the slope and given it a pillowed effect. There is now a great weight of snow to be supported and the risk is higher. If the wind was strong it may have formed a slab, where the snow has been blasted together in one huge lump, making the risk very high.

What time is it?
How much sun has your slope received today? A slope can be safe at 1030, dodgy by midday and downright dangerous by 1330. The avalanche risk changes all the time, just because there are tracks does not mean it is safe.

What is the 'run out' like?
If your slope fans out into a wide gentle area, an avalanche will slow down and spread out reducing your chances of being buried, if it runs into a gully or depression you may be buried under many metres of snow and digging you out could take hours.

3. General tips

- At the start of the day check all transceivers and never take them off during the day.
- Never go off-piste alone. Big groups are also dangerous - four is the ideal size.
- Loosen your backpack and take your hands out of the pole straps
- Only one person should move at a time
- Try to move from one safe spot to another
- Ski down the edges of bowls and not down the middle
- Ski down ridges and spurs rather than bowls and gullies
- Do not bunch up. This places extra stress on the snow pack and weakens it
- Do not ski directly above someone else
- Do not traverse slopes. Never traverse above other skiers.
- Watch and listen for cracks in the snow pack
- Avoid skiing under cornices

Finally, if your assessment has revealed that the slope is too risky then walk away. You may get away with it once or twice, but this approach will eventually get you killed.

[Thanks to Facewest – avalanche specialists for this safety info]

surviving the season

It can be easy to imagine that once you've secured your job then that's it.

You filled in the forms, glammed up your CV, sailed through the interview and got through the months of torment until the season finally started.

Now you're ready to soak up all the pleasure that life can throw at you. Surely from now on it's an endless round of partying and riding for the next five months?

Err...wrong. So you've got there, but of those who start around 20% don't make it to the end.

In some cases it's injury and occasionally family crises that foreshorten the season, but many will either drop out or be sacked, principally because of an information gap – working a ski season actually means *working* a season.

A winter in the Alps is not just a party, it's physically demanding. It might be a world away from sitting in some grey office in a suit and commute lifestyle, but it's still a job, and quite a tough one.

This chapter gives you some insider tips on how to survive your season.

The Training Course

Typically the first few days, or week, of your season will be spent on a training course.

These vary in location and theme, but are usually based in a resort in the Alps and are an opportunity for your employer to bring you up to speed as quickly as possible.

The training course can vary tremendously. One operator's course consisted of a pizza an hour prior to departure topped off with a stark message from the MD limited to 'Just make sure you don't get any complaints!'

More commonly the course will cover a wide range of subjects including guest management, accounts, transfer day, insurance, health & safety and will involve lots of role play.

Bear in mind that although some tour operators let their staff know their resort and/or chalet in advance, others make these decisions during the course. Resort allocations usually depend on an assessment made by senior management leading the course.

When resorts are allocated, don't worry if you get the one resort or chalet everyone was trying to avoid. If you've been chosen to work on your own, it's a mark of confidence in your ability. A bigger resort might sound more fun, but you often get much more out of your season in a smaller community.

And if all of this sounds a bit stressful, we have two important recommendations:

1. Pace Yourself

With all the excitement of being in the Alps after the months of waiting, it can be easy to get carried away.

If you're one of those lucky types who can get hammered and still get up fresh as a daisy in the morning, you're in luck. But this is not the time to sleep through your alarm clock and roll in late.

Every year some staff fail to complete the training course. One chalet girl was dismissed by a tour operator, not for shagging in the bath (hardly encouraged, but not a sackable offence in itself), but for sleeping in the next day.

2. Don't Panic

You've been offered a job because of who you are. Just be yourself...

Once the course is over, you'll then move on to resort, where you will move into your own accommodation, open up your chalet, meet suppliers and generally get ready for your first arrivals.

Ideally, you'll have at least a week to prepare, but it's not unknown to arrive the day before your first guests.

The moral? Pay attention during the training course…!

SURVIVAL TIPS

Under no circumstances should you underestimate how exhausting working a ski season can be.

Playing hard and working hard is tough enough, but living in close proximity with all of your colleagues means that flu and viruses tend to spread like wildfire.

Pretty much everyone who works a season will fall ill at some point, but you can reduce the chances of that and being one of the 20% who fail to complete the season (mainly injuries and sackings), by following our handy tips.

Pace Yourself

At the risk of sounding like your mother, this is the best piece of advice we can offer.

At the start of the season it can be tempting to get on the mountain all day and party all night. Doing this on holiday is hard enough, but try doing it when you've got to get up at 7am six days a week and see how far you get (NB rhetorical, not a challenge!).

Burnout, frequently combined with flu, often hits after New Year. Don't miss January's empty slopes and fresh powder - a night in early doors saves nine (or something like that!).

Work Comes First

Now we definitely sound like your mother! Remember why you are there. It may seem at times that work is simply a tedious obstacle in the way of endless hedonism, but it's worth remembering that without your lift pass, accommodation and weekly beer money, life would be much less entertaining.

Once you stop putting your job first, it's (rubbish pun intended) a slippery slope back to the UK.

Protect Yourself (Pt 1)

But it's not all work, work, work - how about some raunchier advice.

Gather together a large number of young people, away from home, in a holiday atmosphere, mix in lots of alcohol, the fact that 'my place' and 'yours' are only round the corner and the result is a phenomenal amount of sexual activity.

Our recent Sex Survey suggested that workers have an average of four sexual partners per season.

Unfortunately it's not unknown for some staff to leave during the season after falling pregnant – make sure it's not you (or your partner) by using contraception. Condoms are available in all pharmacies and often there's a vending machine on the wall outside to allow for any 'unexpected' requirements.

Have a thick skin

If you are going to indulge, don't expect to have a 'private' life. Gossip is the life-blood of the saisonnier's world. You may well imagine it's just the two of you in on your little 'secret', but do you really know who saw you leave together last night or sneak back home this morning?

More Survival Tips

Protect Yourself (Pt 2)

Suncream is not just for punters. Twenty weeks out in the sun can add years on your looks (for proof of this find any ski instructor over 30 who doesn't need ironing). And you look stupid with a red face.

No Mid-season Blues

Hard as it may be to believe, a routine in the wonderful world of a ski resort is still a routine.

If you don't do transfers, the only time you get out of resort may be to the local supermarket. Enthusiasm can wane and some staff stop skiing and even (shock-horror) going out.

Keep the blues at bay with variety – use your day-off, visit another resort, hitch to the nearest town, try snow-shoeing or telemarking. If still in doubt, look out of the window and remember where you are – it beats office blocks!

Watch the Boozing

Expect to drink a lot. Chalet wine is free and although drinks are not always cheap in bars, what else have you got to spend your money on?

Many chalet girls become G&T addicts and can be sure to end up with a bulging drinks cabinet thanks to all the duty-free that is left behind.

Top tip – crème de cassis makes the chalet white more drinkable.

Punters/Guests/Clients

For all the jokes, your average punter is generally a decent chap, who you will have at least skiing in common with.

This may mean that many dinner conversations start formulaically with 'So where did you ski today?', but if you make the effort most have as many interesting stories tucked away as you.

While some guests you will simply tolerate, most you will like, and a few will even become your friends!

Generally, workers tend to go drinking with colleagues rather than guests. If this is you, tactics can include being vague about where you're going or sneaking out.

Some chalet staff positively encourage socialising with their guests and are highly skilled at engineering it: 'Well, of course, I would come to the pub, but I have all this washing up to do!'

The Journey Out There

- Coach – The most common form of transport. Notionally a great bonding exercise, but only masochists enjoy this 24-hour journey.
- Minibus – Smaller companies often start off in minibus convoy, packed with luggage, mincemeat, Christmas crackers, and with a top speed of 50mph.
- Car - Despite the hassle of insurance (see if your employer will contribute), the risk of accident and the (hopefully loads of) times you'll spend digging your car out of the snow, a car gives you 'freedom'.
- Air - The fortunate (ie working for 'posh' companies or in North America) will fly out to resort. Unfortunately this is the exception to the rule and your allowance will still only be two bags or 20kg.

EVENTS

One way of getting the most out of your season is to make sure you get along to the big events heading your way.

Here are some of the best to look out for:

The Show Love Tour
(www.showlove.co.uk)

There's nothing we like more than 'showing love' to season workers!

The format is simple – Natives takes over a bar or club, puts on a band or a DJ for your entertainment, and hands out free drinks plus vids, DVDs, hoodys, T-shirts, holidays, beanies, skis, boards and whatever else we can get our hands on to make it a full-on party to remember.

The Show Love Tour starts in November at the Daily Mail Ski Show and finishes in May at our Birthday Party. Along the way it takes in over 20 locations in five countries.

ChamJam
(www.chamjam.com)

You need to be in Chamonix in the first week of March for this 'white-knuckle ride and ear-bursting music festival rolled into one'. There are events every day through the week, including Skier and Boarder X, Slopestyle, Big Air and of course…

The Boss des Bosses
(www.natives.co.uk/events/chamjam)

The highlight of the ChamJam week is the Natives sponsored Boss des Bosses. Usually held on the first Wednesday of March, workers from resorts across the Alps descend on Chamonix in their hundreds to support their teams in this inter-resort bumps comp, followed by what usually turns out to be a massive party!

BUSC
(www.busc.net)

BUSC is really a microcosm of a ski season. The only difference is that all the partying and mischief is squeezed into one week and shared out among two thousand students. BUSC is in late-March.

Verbier Ride
(www.verbierride.com)

Held in mid-March, the main event at the Ride is the Big Mountain comp, which doubles up as the British Champs.

FIS & World Cup Races
(www.fis-ski.com)

The FIS circuit runs all year taking in hundreds of resorts and almost every country that has snow. The Downhill is the blue riband event, but slalom races and the fast growing snowboard circuit are both worth going along to see.

Watch out for British stars Leslie McKenna, Alain and Noel Baxter and Chemmy Alcott.

The Natives Workers Challenge
(www.natives.co.uk/race)

Slightly more inclusive than FIS, our own series of races gives all season workers a chance to have a bit of fun.

Each event (held in Méribel, Courchevel and Val d'Isere) includes an individual Giant Slalom and team Parallel Slalom race.

Although some take it seriously, for many it's a chance to dress up (fancy dress is optional) and have a bit of fun - and for everyone it's another great excuse for a party!

Other events to watch out for include

- The Brits (Deux Alpes)
- Snowbombing (Villars)
- The Burton European Open (Livigno)
- Luttman-Johnson Race (Zermatt)
- Gumby's Big Day Out (Val d'Isère)
- Derby de la Meije (La Grave)
- Red Bull Extreme (Verbier)
- UFO Snowboarding Champs (Arinsal)

post-season

All through the season, the question you'll be asked more than any other is 'What do you do in the summer?'

After a while you're so used to being asked, it's easy for some slight exaggerations to sneak in ("I'm an indoor hang-gliding instructor" is the best we've heard), but as the season creeps on, what was once a joke suddenly becomes deadly serious.

By the end of March, what you do in the summer – specifically the one fast approaching – becomes much more relevant.

What do you do when the season ends? How to avoid post-season gloom? Does it all really end? We help you extend the season for as long as you want…

Reunions

From around the middle of March, you'll start talking about what'll happen when it all ends. By the time April comes around you'll be wondering if you'll ever see these people you've spent all your season with again.

The good news is that the partying keeps on going through May with loads of official and unofficial reunion parties.

In the last few years Natives has been involved in organising end-of-season parties from Glasgow to London, featuring DJs, bands, drinks promotions and lots of prizes to win.

Natives/GJs Reunions

Some of the most popular take place during the first few weekends of May at GJs, a snow-friendly pub (it's owned by the owner of the original GJs in Val d'Isere) in south-west London.

These nights feature the best bands from the winter, which in recent years has included Fourplay, The Noize, Superfly, Shibboleth and Bluefunkt.

GJ's SW18

Natives Birthday Party

Rather like the Queen, we have a couple of birthdays – the official one, and the one with the big party!

The big party is usually held in the last week of May/first week of June and tends to be a HUGE night out, with thousands of pounds worth of prizes and lots of free drinks. 2004 will be our 5th Birthday Party – so expect something special!

Tips for Reunions

- Don't organise it too soon, or you'll have nothing to say
- Don't organise it too late, or you'll miss those going travelling and/or doing summer seasons
- It may be predictable, but London tends to be the easiest for everyone to get to
- Bring your season pics with you
- Be prepared to be spun out by the sight of familiar faces in an unfamiliar setting

Summer Seasons

One question you'll hear more than any other during your winter season is "What do you do in the summer?"

Guests tend to assume that workers permanently flit from one season to the next. But it's not such a stupid question – after the winter in the mountains, the thought of British weather, desk jobs, and tiring commutes may not be enough to tempt you back.

Fortunately both Natives and our sister site ResortJobs (www.resortjobs.co.uk) list lots of summer jobs from as early as November or December.

Beach Resorts

A large proportion of summer jobs are in beach resorts throughout Europe. Beware though – some of these jobs will overlap with the ski season, as the summer season begins early in countries like Greece, Turkey and Cyprus. In countries like Spain, France and Portugal, the season begins just after the winter season ends, so don't expect to have too much time off in between!

Opportunities exist for reps, resort managers, watersports and activity instructors, nannies and childrens representatives, bar and hotel staff, chefs, villa host/esses, and various others.

Lakes and Mountains

Many ski companies operate a smaller programme in summer, with jobs available for chalet staff, reps and nannies.

Don't underestimate the appeal of Alpine resorts during the summer months – the mountains look just as good without snow, and there are heaps of activities on offer, including mountain biking, walking, paragliding, rafting, canyoning, and most outdoor pursuits.

Seasons in Alpine areas are shorter, and run from around mid-June until mid-September.

Campsites

Several tour operators specialise in self-drive camping holidays for families, and have many job opportunities, including campsite reps, childrens reps, and supervisory roles. There are jobs available in France, Spain, and Italy.

Many of the staff are employed to erect tents and set up equipment prior to the beginning of the season, and can begin as early as the beginning of March, but it is still possible to begin contracts in May, ending in September/October.

Activity Centres

There are a number of these in the UK and in Europe, providing adventure holidays for children in large residential activity centres.

Positions include catering staff, activity instructors, reps and group leaders, management staff, and administrators.

Staff are employed from April through to September, although there are many short-term positions available, and applications are welcomed from anyone who can commit to at least eight weeks.

Yachts

Some winter staff go on and work on private yachts for the summer – great if you can get it, with excellent wages on offer and glamorous locations.

Be warned though – competition for yacht work is extremely fierce, and most positions are for very experienced chefs/cooks. The best way to find something is to head to Antibes at the beginning of April, and talk to the specialist agencies there, ensuring you have an up to date CV and references.

'Cold-calling' on boats can be successful, but be prepared for lots of knock backs. There will be plenty of others searching for work, so be persistent, and ensure you have enough money to support yourself while you search.

Barges

Several operators offer barging holidays in the UK and in Europe, so there are a small number of vacancies on offer, with positions including bar staff, host/hostess, and tour guide. Barge experience is usually not necessary but previous hospitality experience is required, and for tour guide positions, language skills are necessary.

The season is relatively short, with positions available from June until September.

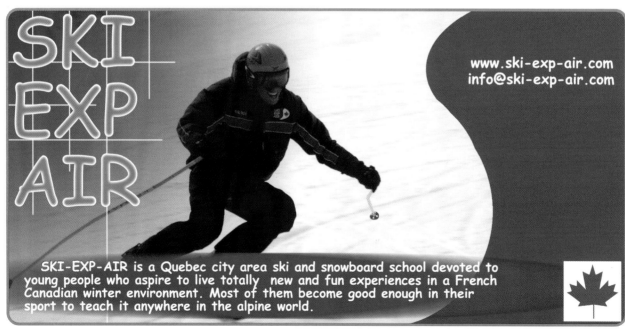

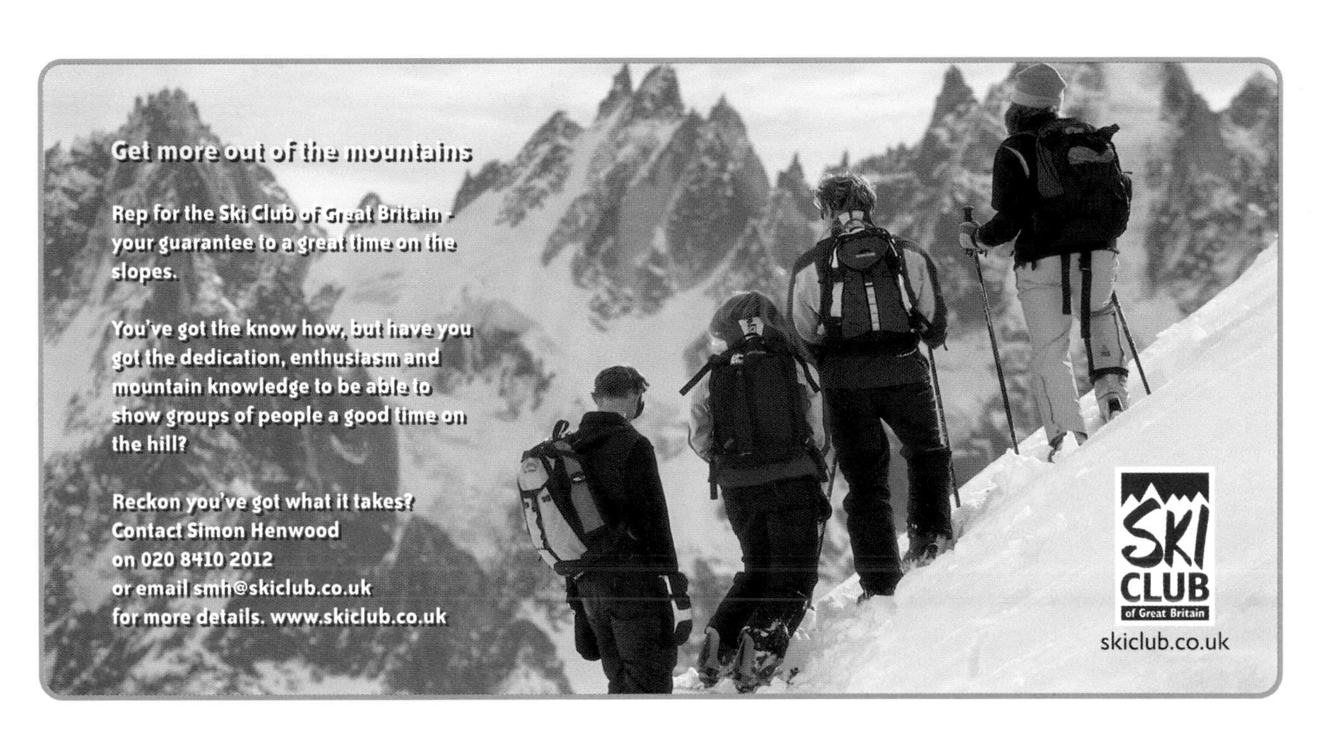
Get more out of the mountains
Rep for the Ski Club of Great Britain - your guarantee to a great time on the slopes.
You've got the know how, but have you got the dedication, enthusiasm and mountain knowledge to be able to show groups of people a good time on the hill?
Reckon you've got what it takes?
Contact Simon Henwood
on 020 8410 2012
or email smh@skiclub.co.uk
for more details. www.skiclub.co.uk
SKI CLUB
of Great Britain
skiclub.co.uk

MORIS
PUB

ROND POINT

DORON
PUB

The MOUNTAIN TRADING COMPANY owns & manages the Moris Pub (Val d'Isère), the Doron Pub, Scott's and the Rond Point (Méribel) and La Terrasse (Chamonix). We recruit up to 100 staff each winter. We look for dedicated, hard-working staff with excellent customer service skills. Full training is provided for all positions. Applications are considered from August and interviews are held in London in September and October. To apply please visit www.mountaintradingco.com, print out and complete an application form and send by post to:

Mountain Trading Company, c/o Mark Warner, George House, 61-65 Kensington Church Street, London W8 4BA.

SCOTT'S
RESTAURANT • BAR

CAFE
LA TERRASSE

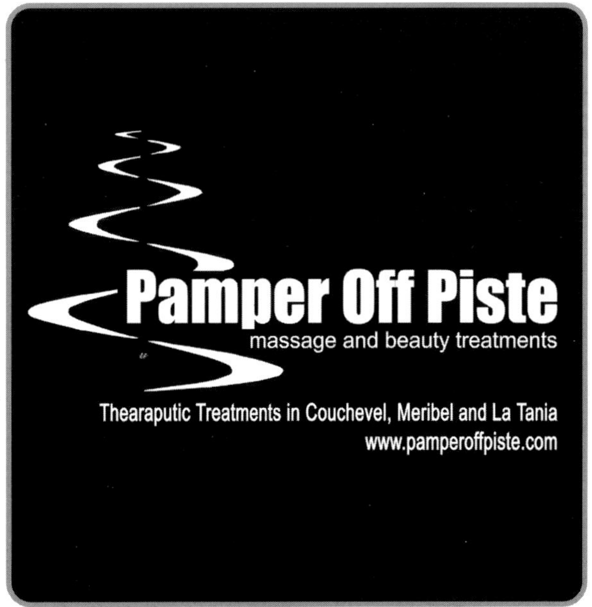
Pamper Off Piste
massage and beauty treatments
Thearaputic Treatments in Couchevel, Meribel and La Tania
www.pamperoffpiste.com

Small, quality independent ski company, specialists to Vaujany / Alpe d'Huez, require friendly and professional staff for their catered chalets, hotels and apartments.

www.skipeak.com

Applicants should be at least 21 years of age and can send their CV and covering note via email to nigel@skipeak.com

Powder Byrne is THE professional ski company, providing 1st class holidays to the Alps. resort opportunities for the full season or shorter periods as: Resort Mgrs, Ski Guides, Drivers & Children's Club staff.

Package includes: accom, flights, ins, ski pass, ski equip, and salary. Apply on-line at: www.powderbyrne.com

Cordon Rouge
Specialist chalet catering company, operating in French Alps for over 20 years

Dicks Tea Bar Group
Leisure group incorporating Dicks Tea Bar, La Taverne, and Pizza Express

Equity Travel
One of UK's leading independent tour operators

Esprit Holidays
20 years' experience providing excellent service for quality family holidays

First Choice
Leading wintersports operator, providing a variety of snowsport holidays

Interski
Specialising in group and family holidays in the Aosta valley for 19 years

Le Ski
Family run company, with chalets in Val d'Isere, La Tania and Courchevel

Meriski
The Méribel expert. Our 17 chalets are amongst the finest in Méribel

NBV Leisure
Providing resort services with a range of tour operators in popular resorts

PGL Travel
Europe's largest provider of adventure holidays for children

Purple Ski
Privately owned company providing quality catered chalet holidays in Méribel

Simon Butler Skiing
Entering 20th season, offering quality ski instructional holidays in Mègeve

Simply Travel
Superb chalet holidays of the highest quality in some of the world's most sought-after resorts

Ski Beat
Small, friendly company with chalets in La Plagne, Les Arcs, La Tania & Val d'Isère

Ski Olympic
Family-run tour operator, providing skiing holidays for 18 years

Ski Total
21st season providing quality ski holidays

Ski Val
Independent family business, with over 25 years specialist experience

Snowline/VIP
Small friendly ski company with catered chalets in Val d'Isère, Méribel, La Tania and Morzine

The Ski Company
Superlative chalets in Méribel, Val d'Isère, Zermatt, and Verbier

DRY/SNOW SLOPES

Ackers Trust Ski Centre, Birmingham
0121 772 5111

Aldershot, Hants
01252 325 889

Bearsden Ski and Board, Glasgow
0141 943 1500

Capel Curig, Gwynedd
01690 720214

Chatham, Kent
01634 827979

Gloucester Ski and Snowboard Centre
01452 414300

Hemel Ski Centre, Herts
01442 241321

Lecht Ski Centre, Strathdon
01975 651440

Midlothian Ski Centre, Edinburgh
0131 445 4433

Rossendale Ski Centre, Lancs
01706 226457

Sheffield Ski Village, S Yorks
0114 276 9459

Stoke Ski Centre, Staffs
01782 204159

Swadlincote, Derbys
01283 217200

Tamworth Snowdome, Staffs
0990 00 00 11

Wycombe Summit, Berks
01494 474711

Xscape Snowdome, Milton Keynes
01908 200 020

More at www.natives.co.uk/dryski.htm

ALPINE INTERNET CAFES

Arinsal, Andorra - Ciber Café
www.cibercafeandorra.com
00 376 839683

Chamonix, France - I-Guest
I-guest@euroscan.com
04 50 55 98 58

Chamonix, France - CyBar
cybarchamonix@hotmail.com
04 50 53 64 80

Courchevel 1850, France - WebSki
moutcha@moutcha.com
04 79 01 01 01

Courchevel 1650, France - Le Bubble
www.lebubble.com
04 79 01 14 21

La Clusaz, France - Pub Le Salto
www.publesalto.com
04 50 63 37 01

Les Deux Alpes, France - Smokey Joes
www.smokeyjoes.fr
04 76 79 28 97

Méribel, France - CyBar
cybarmeribel@hotmail.com
06 17 74 43 73

Morzine, France - Yodelnet Cafe
Opposite the Rex Cinema

St Anton, Austria - Mailbox
www.mail-box.at
06 99 1002 2001

Steamboat Springs, USA - Geeks Garage
www.geeksgarage.com
879 2976

Sauze d'Oulx, Italy - Sporting Club Valsusa
info@sportingclubvalsusa.com

Val d'Isere, France - Powdermonkey
pat@powdermonkey.co.uk
04 79 06 62 29

Whistler, Canada - Jodys
www.jodys.ca
604 932 8380

www.natives.co.uk/places/cafes.htm

BARS

Chamonix - The Jekyll
www.thejekyll.com

Chamonix - La Terrasse
natives.co.uk/bars/cha/terrasse.htm

Chamonix - Wild Wallabies
natives.co.uk/bars/cha/wallaby.htm

Courchevel 1650 - Le Bubble
www.lebubble.fr

La Tania - Pub Le Ski Lodge
www.publeskilodge.com

Les Deux Alpes - Smokey Joes
www.smokeyjoes.fr

Les Deux Alpes - Smithys
natives.co.uk/bars/lda/smithys.htm

Méribel - Le Doron Pub
natives.co.uk/bars/mer/pub.htm

Méribel - Le Rond Point
natives.co.uk/bars/mer/rondpoint.htm

Méribel - La Tsaretta
natives.co.uk/bars/mer/tsaretta.htm

Méribel Village - Lodge du Village
natives.co.uk/bars/mer/lodge.htm

Serre Chevalier - Le LB Bar
natives.co.uk/bars/ser/lbbar.htm

Tignes - TCs Bar
www.tcsbar.com

Val d'Isere - Café Fats
natives.co.uk/bars/tig/tcs.htm

Val d'Isere - Moris Pub
natives.co.uk/bars/val/moris.htm

Val d'Isere - Le Petit Danois
natives.co.uk/bars/val/danois.htm

More at www.natives.co.uk/bars